Scholastic's
The Magic School Bus®
INSIDE RALPHIE
A Book About Germs

JACKSON ELEMENTARY SCHOOL

Scholastic Inc.
New York Toronto London Auckland Sydney

From an episode of the animated TV series
produced by Scholastic Productions, Inc.
Based on *The Magic School Bus* books
written by Joanna Cole and illustrated by Bruce Degen.

Based upon an episode of The Magic School Bus TV series
by John May and Jocelyn Stevenson,
illustrated by John Speirs

Library of Congress Cataloging-in-Publication Data

The Magic school bus inside Ralphie: a book about germs.
p.   cm.
Written by Beth Nadler and illustrated by John Speirs.
1. Infection — Juvenile literature. 2. Natural immunity — Juvenile
literature. [1. Infection. 2. Immunity.] I. Nadler, Beth.
RC113.M24   1995
616.07'9 — dc20   94-44655
CIP
AC

ISBN 0-590-40025-8

24 23 22   2/0

Printed in the U.S.A.   24

First Scholastic printing, May 1995

Having a teacher like Ms. Frizzle can make a kid nervous. Strange things always seem to happen when she's around. Take last week, when our class was supposed to do a live TV show for the Frizzle News Network. Ralphie was going to come up with an exciting story for us to cover. But here it was, Broadcast Day, and Ralphie was nowhere to be found.

Everyone was getting worried.

"We can't do it without him," Wanda said in a panic. She stared at the door, hoping Ralphie would race in. But he didn't. Instead, the telephone rang.

"Oh, yes. I see. He's sick. Poor Ralphie!" Ms. Frizzle said into the phone. "Of course he must stay in bed."

Carlos tried to get Ms. Frizzle's attention. "What about Broadcast Day?" he asked.

"Why, we're taking the school to him," Ms. Frizzle replied as she hung up the phone. "To the bus!" she ordered us.

Here we go again.

I *think* I should have stayed home!

As we boarded the bus we began to get worried. This seemed an awful lot like one of Ms. Frizzle's strange field trip ideas.

"Ms. Frizzle, are you sure this visit isn't a field trip?" Arnold asked finally.

Ms. Frizzle just grinned. "What do *you* think, Arnold?"

Ms. Frizzle closed the door and turned the key in the ignition. Boy, was Ralphie about to be surprised!

Ralphie was home in bed getting ready to take his medicine.

"How can anything that smells like grape shoe polish help my body get well?" Ralphie asked his mother, who just happened to be a doctor.

"It will if you take one teaspoon three times a day," she replied. "Now I have to go see a patient. Grampa's downstairs if you need anything. I'll check in later."

Ralphie knew his mom wanted him to rest. But how could he rest, knowing he'd let everyone down on Broadcast Day? He jumped out of bed and went over to his computer. Maybe if he came up with a really great idea for the news show he could phone it in to the classroom. But even walking over to the computer made him tired.

Just then, Ralphie saw us all standing right there on his sidewalk. He looked very surprised!

We followed Ms. Frizzle straight up to Ralphie's bedroom.
"We came to do Broadcast Day," Wanda told Ralphie.
"What a great idea!" Ralphie exclaimed.
"Now and then I do have them." Ms. Frizzle laughed.

"Cough. Cough. Cough." Ralphie's cold was getting worse.

"You'd better take it easy, Ralphie," said Ms. Frizzle. "Your body is telling you to s-l-o-w d-o-w-n."

"But Ms. Frizzle! I can't. We have a show to do. What does my body know, anyway?" Ralphie asked.

That's when Ms. Frizzle got that look on her face — the one that makes us nervous. "It knows a lot about the detection and rejection of infection, Ralphie. Inside you, at this moment, there is action! Adventure! Excitement!"

Ralphie's a pony.
Get it?
He's a little hoarse!

Carlos, your jokes are making *us* sick!

I wonder if Ralphie looks as sick ins[ide]
as he does outside.

The Friz ordered us all back on the bus. Suddenly we were getting smaller. Helicopter blades whirred over our heads. The Magic School Bus had become a Magic School Helicopter.

"What's going on?" Ralphie shouted over the noise.

"We're here to get the inside story," answered Ms. Frizzle.

"Seat belts everyone!" Ms. Frizzle called back to us. "Ralphie, say 'Ahhhh.'"

Ralphie opened his mouth wide. We flew right down his throat. It was red and swollen. The bus must have tickled going down, because Ralphie coughed — hard. The bus flew back out of his mouth.

What's going on?

Whooaaah!

We had to find another way to get inside Ralphie's body. "I've got it!" Ralphie cried out excitedly. "Look at this!"

He peeled off a bandage to show us a cut on his leg. We could enter through it. But the bus had to be even *smaller* to dive into a teeny tiny cut.

We were inside Ralphie. But we were nowhere near his sore throat.

"Could we travel through his bloodstream to get to his sore throat?" asked Dorothy Ann.

"Absolutely!" answered Ms. Frizzle.

Ralphie watched us on his TV as we floated along in a thin, clear liquid.

"Is that my blood?" Ralphie asked. "I thought blood was red. That stuff is clear."

"The liquid part of the blood is clear," Ms. Frizzle explained.

"So what are those red things?" Ralphie asked.

Dorothy Ann opened her notebook. "According to my research, they're called red blood cells. And the white ones are called white blood cells."

"Red blood cells carry oxygen to all parts of the body," Keesha added. "White blood cells search out and destroy germs. Platelets help the body heal scrapes and cuts."

Just then, Ralphie's mother came back to check on him. That's when she spotted us on the TV!

"What's that you're watching?" she asked. "It's remarkably realistic."

Ralphie had to think fast — he couldn't let his mother know where the class really was! "Those are just cheap TV special effects. Look, you can even see the wires!" he said.

The bus jerked to a stop. "We're here in the throat!" Ms. Frizzle called out. "It's time for some on-the-spot reporting."

Keesha and Carlos took one camera, Phoebe and Arnold took another. They quickly scrambled off the bus.

"Look at that, folks! Have we got us some action!" Carlos said in his best news reporter voice. "Those yellow-green balls are alive. They're destroying that wall!"

The yellow-green balls were bacteria cells. They were attacking Ralphie's throat. The bacteria were the bad guys that were making Ralphie sick.

"According to my research, bacteria are germs," Dorothy Ann explained. "Once inside our bodies, they can make us sick."

Back at the scene of the infection, Carlos noticed a lot of white blood cells. The white blood cells attacked the bacteria. The battle was on and for a moment it seemed as though the white blood cells would win.

Then, the bacteria began to divide! There were four, then eight, then more and more! There were too many bacteria for the white blood cells to battle on their own!

As he watched the action on the TV, Ralphie got scared. "How could my body lose?"

"I don't think you should be watching this," Ralphie's mom said with concern. She got up to leave. "Your body needs to save its strength so it can use its energy to battle those bacteria."

Believe me! You *need rest!*

Oh no! I feel worse.

The bacteria were everywhere! The reporters found themselves stuck in the middle of the battle! "Ralphie! *Where's our backup support?"* Dorothy Ann shouted.

"B-backup support?" Ralphie said weakly. "Where do I get that?"

"It's already on its way," said Ms. Frizzle calmly.

Just then, a river of purple fluid washed past the bus.

"Looks like grape shoe polish," Carlos said.

But it wasn't grape shoe polish. It was the medicine Ralphie had taken earlier.

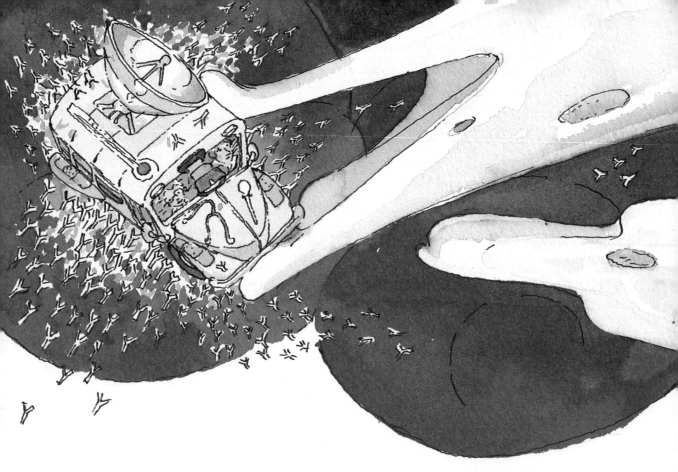

The medicine worked side by side with the white blood cells to destroy the bacteria.

"It's destroying more bacteria!" Tim cheered. "The medicine is giving the white blood cells a chance!"

Just then a white blood cell sprayed antibodies all over the bus! It's the antibodies' job to mark bacteria. That's how the white blood cells know what to attack.

"Ralphie's white blood cells are doing such a good job!" Ms. Frizzle announced. "They now recognize us as enemies, too."

"Enemies?" Arnold gulped. "But we know what white blood cells do to enemies!"

Ms. Frizzle smiled. "They'll try to destroy us. Ah, the wonder of the human body."

Now we were really scared! We cried for Ralphie to help us, but he was fast asleep.

"Don't worry class," Ms. Frizzle said. "In order to destroy us, Ralphie's white blood cells will have to catch us."

She put her foot on the bus's gas pedal. We zoomed through Ralphie's body!

The bus made a sharp turn. Ms. Frizzle spoke into the broadcast microphone. "Ms. Frizzle here with an update on the Ralphie story," she said. "To escape the white blood cells, we have left Ralphie's throat and are now heading up his nasal passages."

"His what?" Keesha whispered to Dorothy Ann.

Dorothy Ann flipped through her science book. "According to my research, that means his nose!"

Well, there were a lot of places we would have rather been, but at least we were away from those white blood cells!

We're up Ralphie's nose? Blech!

It was getting late. We had to get back to school. But we were stuck in Ralphie's nose. There was only one thing to do. Ralphie was going to have to sneeze us out!

The bus flew out of Ralphie's nose and landed safely in a soft pile of socks.

"So, Ralphie," Keesha said, shoving her news microphone into Ralphie's face, "what do you have to say about today's exciting adventure?"

"I'm sorry my body made such a mess of it," Ralphie croaked.

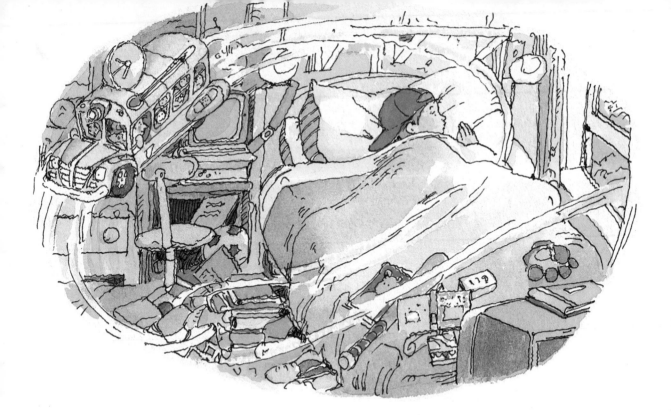

"Your body's built to keep out things like a bunch of germs — or a bus of kids," Wanda explained to him.

"Okay," Ralphie agreed. "But what about when you almost got gobbled up by my white blood cells?"

The memory made Arnold shiver. "Only because your body thought we were bacteria," he said.

"That's the inside story, Ralphie," Ms. Frizzle said. Then she ordered everyone back on the bus. It was time to let Ralphie rest.

"We may have won the battle," she said. "But Ralphie's still fighting the war."

Letters from Our Readers

(Editor's note: They will help you tell what is real
and what is make-believe in this story.)

Dear Editor:

Ralphie shouldn't have pulled a bandage off his cut. If the Magic School Bus got in, so could germs!

Signed,

Always Undercover

Dear Editor:

I know there's a lot you can do to keep from getting sick, like eating right, getting enough sleep, and exercising. But what I don't know is does Ms. Frizzle ever get sick?

Signed,

Friz Fan

My school bus driver once got lost and we wound up in the next town! But we never wound up inside someone's body. Those kids are lucky they only ran into one kind of germ. They could have had to battle fungi, parasites, or viruses. They can make you sick, too.

Your pal,

Lost and Found

Dear Friz Fan:

Ms. Frizzle never gets sick. Ever.

The Editor

Dear Kids, Parents, and Teachers

Your body is always working to keep you healthy. When you get sick, it works even harder to get you well. Your skin helps keep germs out of your body. The tiny hairs in your nose trap germs. The fluids in your nose and throat continually wash germs away. So do the tears in your eyes.

Sometimes germs do get into your body and grow despite your body's efforts. That is when you get sick. Your body fights germs in many ways. Even fever, swelling, and achiness may help your body contain the spread of germs and overcome them. Medicines work with your body's natural defenses to destroy germs.

When all the germs in your body that make you sick are destroyed, you get well again.

Ms. Frizzle